W9-BRD-227

Smithsonian

LITTLE EXPLORER

African Animals

by Martha E. H. Rustad

CAPSTONE PRESS
a capstone imprint

Little Explorer is published by Capstone Press,
1710 Roe Crest Drive, North Mankato, Minnesota 56003
www.capstonepub.com

The name of the Smithsonian Institution and the sunburst logo
are registered trademarks of the Smithsonian Institution.
For more information, please visit www.si.edu.

Library of Congress Cataloging-in-Publication Data
Rustad, Martha E. H. (Martha Elizabeth Hillman), 1975– author.

African animals / by Martha E. H. Rustad.
    pages cm. — (Smithsonian little explorer)
  Summary: "Introduces types of animals found in Africa and
African habitats to young readers"—Provided by publisher.
  Audience: Grade K to 3.
  Audience: 4-8.
Includes index.
  ISBN 978-1-4765-3933-1 (library binding)
  ISBN 978-1-4765-5181-4 (paperback)
  ISBN 978-1-4765-5269-9 (paper over board)
1. Animals—Africa—Juvenile literature. I. Title.

QL336.R92 2014
591.96—dc23   2013032349

Editorial Credits
Kristen Mohn, editor; Sarah Bennett, designer; Marcie Spence,
media researcher; Danielle Ceminsky, production specialist

Our very special thanks to Dr. Don E. Wilson, Curator Emeritus
of the Department of Vertebrate Zoology, National Museum of
Natural History, Smithsonian Institution, for his curatorial review.
Capstone would also like to thank Kealy Wilson, Smithsonian
Institution Project Coordinator and Product Development
Manager, and the following at Smithsonian Enterprises: Ellen
Nanney, Licensing Manager; Brigid Ferraro, Director of Licensing;
Carol LeBlanc, Senior Vice President, Consumer & Education
Products.

Image Credits
Alamy Images: FLPA, 24, Mark Bowler, 15 (bottom), Picture Press,
13 (bottom), Ray Wilson, 21 (middle); Getty Images: Beverly
Joubert, 23 (top left), De Agostini Picture Library, 25 (top), Millard
H Sharp, 16 (bottom); Minden Pictures: Mark Newman, 27 (top);
Nature Picture Library: Jose B. Ruiz, 25 (bottom); Shutterstock:
Aliaksandr Radzko, design element, Alta Oosthuizen, 19 (top),
Anton_Ivanov, 2-3, 32, Cattallina, design element, EcoPrint,
12, 16 (top), erichon, 29, FAUP, 15 (top), Fir4ik, design element,
Grobler du Preez, 5 (top left), Hedrus, 8-9, Heiko Kiera, 23 (bottom
right), Hein Nouwens, design element, Henrik Larsson, 21
(bottom), InnaFelker, 26 (inset), Jasper_Lensseling_Photography,
21 (top), javarman, 19 (middle), Johan Swanepoel, 8 (bottom), Jo
Crebbin, 18 (left), Jordan Tan, 7 (top left), Josep Pena Llorens, 28,
Leslie Crookes, 11 (bottom), lupulluss, design element, Marek
Velechovsky, 23 (bottom left), Mogens Trolle, 10 (bottom), Naiyyer,
5 (top right), Liew Weng Keong, 20, niall dunne, 1, Nico Traut, 27
(bottom), NSemprevivo, 18 (bottom right), Oded Ben-Raphael, 22
(inset), Oleg Znamenskiy, 6 (top), Pal Teravagimov, 19 (bottom),
PeterVrabel, 23 (top right), Peter Schwarz, 13 (top), Photocreo
Michal Bednarek, 4-5, Pichugin Dmitry, 26 (back), PRILL, 30-31,
Sam DCruz, 6 (bottom), Sergey Uryadnikov, 17, Stacey Ann
Alberts, 7 (bottom right), Stephen N Haynes, 14, tristan tan, design
element, Villiers Steyn, 22 (back), Volodymyr Burdiak, cover,
zixian, 10-11

For SPCL, intrepid explorers. —MEHR

Printed in the United States of America in Stevens Point, Wisconsin.
092013   007769WZS14

TABLE OF CONTENTS

SAFARI!

Vast grasslands, thick rain forests, dry deserts, busy waters. Animals find homes in many African habitats.

Tiny tsetse flies flit. Enormous elephants ramble. Let's go on a safari around Africa.

Long eyelashes protect a camel's eyes from desert sand.

It can close its nose too.

Camels help people travel across wide deserts. A camel can live as long as seven days without drinking water.

A safari is a trip to look at wild animals in their natural homes.

HERBIVORES

The savanna is full of grasses and small trees. These plants are food for the herbivores. Herbivores are animals that eat plants.

Gazelles graze early in the morning. They get water from the plants they eat.

Impalas run fast and jump high to escape from enemies. They live in large herds of about 100.

The variety of herbivores helps the savanna grasses grow. Each animal eats different grasses at different stages.

Tall giraffes eat leaves from acacia trees. Their long tongues pull on the thorny plants.

Adults eat up to 145 pounds (66 kilograms) of food each day.

Giraffes must spread their front legs wide to reach water to drink.

More than 90 kinds of antelopes wander here.

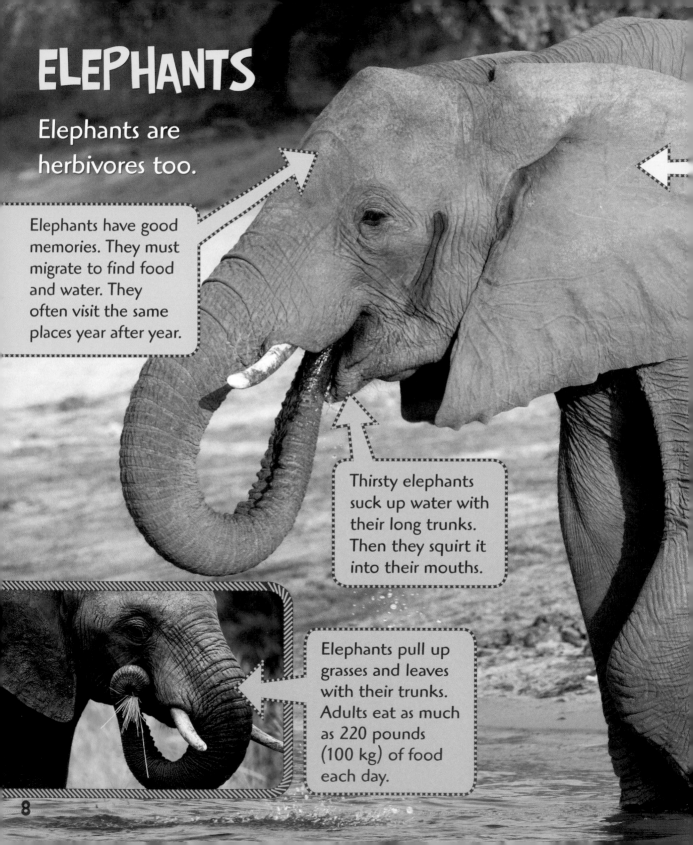

ELEPHANTS

Elephants are herbivores too.

Elephants have good memories. They must migrate to find food and water. They often visit the same places year after year.

Thirsty elephants suck up water with their long trunks. Then they squirt it into their mouths.

Elephants pull up grasses and leaves with their trunks. Adults eat as much as 220 pounds (100 kg) of food each day.

Elephants can hear each other up to 6 miles (10 kilometers) away.

AFRICAN CATS

A pride of lions lives together in the savanna. Prides have one or more males, about 10 females, and all their cubs.

Teams of females hunt zebras, antelopes, and wildebeests. The lions crouch behind plants and pounce on prey.

The full cats doze in the grass after eating.

Lions are carnivores. Carnivores hunt and eat animals.

A leopard may carry prey into a tree to eat. It rests on a branch after a big meal.

SPEEDY FELINES

African cat species	top speed
cheetahs	71 miles (114 km) per hour
caracals	50 miles (80 km) per hour
servals	50 miles (80 km) per hour
lions	40 miles (64 km) per hour
leopards	36 miles (58 km) per hour

DOGS IN AFRICA

Jackals hunt at night.

They sometimes follow prides of lions. Jackals eat the lions' leftovers.

Jackals also eat plants and bugs.

Spotted hyenas are not picky eaters.

They scavenge food that other animals leave behind.

Hyenas' sharp eyes see prey well at night. Their barks sound like laughter.

PRIMATES

Primates are a group of mammals including apes, monkeys, and humans.

Many primates live in the rain forest. Tall trees and vines grow in this wet habitat.

Gorillas are a type of ape. They live together in small groups.

Gorillas eat leaves and fruit during the day. Every night they build a new nest for sleeping.

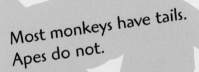

Most monkeys have tails. Apes do not.

Talapoin monkeys live in large groups. They climb trees and swim in rivers. They store food in their cheek pouches.

Bush babies live in rain forest trees. They jump from tree to tree.

At night their big eyes watch for predators.

Bush babies use their sharp teeth to poke holes in trees. They suck out a sticky liquid called gum.

Bonobos groom each other's fur and pick out bugs.

They sometimes groom and play with monkeys.

16

Bonobos climb trees to find fruit.

BIRDS

Look up! Birds fill the skies over Africa.

Many birds migrate there during winter. Other birds stay all year.

flamingos

Ostriches run across the African savanna. They do not fly. They are too big. Ostriches grow as tall as 9 feet (2.7 meters).

Ostrich eggs are the biggest eggs in the world.

Vultures find and eat dead animals.

Vultures spot food from high above with sharp eyes. Their strong beaks rip the food apart.

INSECTS

Colorful butterflies
fly in the rain forest.

Eyed pansy butterflies
have bright orange
spots on their wings.

Dung beetles roll animal dung into balls. They lay eggs in the dung.

Don't forget bug spray on safari. Some insects make humans and animals sick.

Mosquito bites can spread malaria. Bites from tiny tsetse flies can give humans and animals sleeping sickness.

tsetse fly

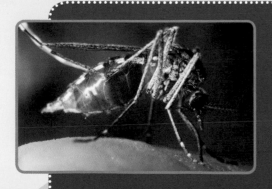

DEADLY BITES

Which African animal is the deadliest? The answer may surprise you: the mosquito. According to the World Health Organization, malaria causes more than 1 million deaths each year.

REPTILES

Reptiles live in Africa's rivers, deserts, and rain forests.

Nile crocodiles lay in the sun on riverbanks. Their bodies grow up to 20 feet (6 m) long.

Only their eyes show when they float in the river. Splash! Crocodiles pull their prey underwater.

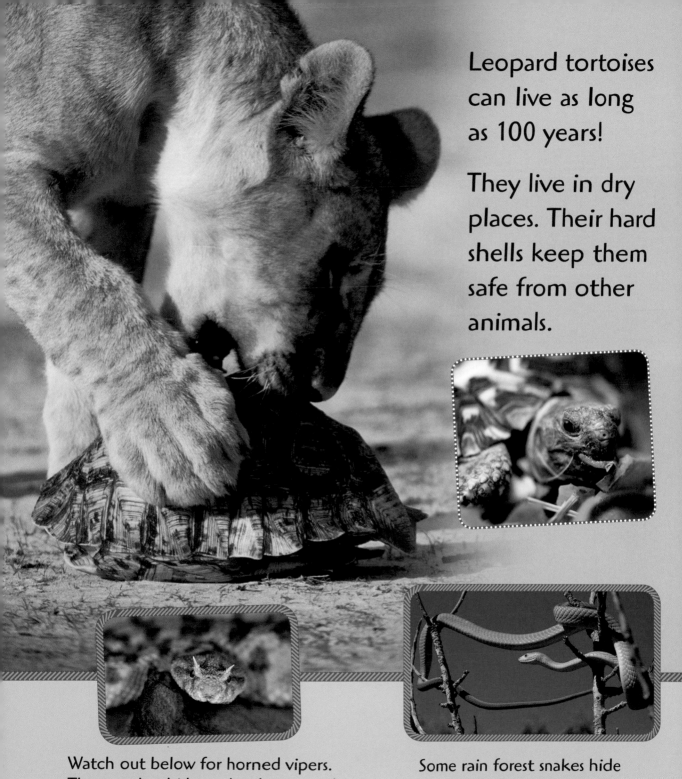

Leopard tortoises can live as long as 100 years!

They live in dry places. Their hard shells keep them safe from other animals.

Watch out below for horned vipers. These snakes hide under desert sand. They surprise and bite their prey.

Some rain forest snakes hide overhead. Green mambas hunt birds in tree branches.

AMPHIBIANS

Amphibians live in water and on land.

Red-banded rubber frogs hide all day on the savanna. At night they eat ants and termites.

They can even flip their sticky tongues behind their heads to catch prey.

Hairy frogs grow extra
skin near their legs.
The skin looks like hair.
It helps the frogs breathe.

Salamanders live only in coastal
parts of northern Africa.
The sharp-ribbed salamander
pushes poisonous spines out
its sides to keep safe.

WATER ANIMALS

Our last safari stop is underwater.

More than 200 kinds of fish swim in Lake Victoria and the Nile River.

The salty ocean water around Africa is home to many animals as well.

Victoria Falls

Look in shallow ponds for African lungfish. They stay alive even if the pond dries up in the heat.

Lungfish push mucus out of their skin. It protects them for up to a year in dry weather.

Southern right whales migrate to Africa from Antarctica. They find food and safe places to have their young.

CONSERVATION

Conservation means working to keep natural habitats safe.

People and animals must live together on this vast continent.

Hunters sometimes kill animals for food or to stay safe. But wildlife parks protect animals.

Many people travel to Africa every year to see animals.

THANK YOU FOR COMING ON AN **AFRICAN SAFARI!**

GLOSSARY

acacia—a thorny tree or bush that has white or yellow flowers

amphibian—a cold-blooded animal with a backbone; amphibians live in water when young and can live on land as adults

carnivore—an animal that eats meat

conservation—the protection of animals and plants, as well as the wise use of what we get from nature

continent—one of Earth's seven large landmasses

dung—solid waste from animals

groom—to keep clean; apes and monkeys groom each other by picking bugs off each other's fur

habitat—the natural place and conditions in which a plant or animal lives

herbivore—an animal that eats plants

herd—a large group of animals that lives or moves together

malaria—a serious disease that people get from mosquito bites

migrate—to travel from one area to another on a regular basis

mucus—a slimy, thick fluid

poisonous—able to harm or kill with poison or venom

predator—an animal that hunts other animals for food

prey—an animal hunted by another animal for food

pride—a group or family of lions

rain forest—a thick forest where rain falls almost every day

reptile—a cold-blooded animal that breathes air and has a backbone; most reptiles lay eggs and have scaly skin

safari—a trip to view wild animals in their natural homes, usually in Africa

savanna—a flat, grassy area of land with few or no trees

scavenge—to feed on dead animals or plants

sleeping sickness—a serious disease that tsetse flies spread

tsetse fly—an African fly that sucks blood of humans and other mammals

wildebeest—a large African animal with a head like an ox, two curved horns, and a long tail

CRITICAL THINKING USING THE COMMON CORE

Look at the camel photo on page 5. List three things about the animal that help it live in the desert. (Key Ideas and Details)

Find the Speedy Felines chart on page 11. Which cat is the fastest? Explain what you can learn about African cats from studying the chart. (Craft and Structure)

What item does the author say to bring on safari? Why is this item important? What else would you want to bring? (Integration of Ideas and Knowledge)

READ MORE

Allgor, Marie. *Endangered Animals of Africa.* Save Earth's Animals! New York: PowerKids Press, 2011.

Lindeen, Mary. *Lions.* My First Animal Library, Zoo Animals. Minneapolis: Jump!, 2014.

Rustad, Martha E. H. *Zebras and Oxpeckers Work Together.* Animals Working Together. Mankato, Minn.: Capstone Press, 2011.

INTERNET SITES

FactHound offers a safe, fun way to find Internet sites related to this book. All of the sites on FactHound have been researched by our staff.

Here's all you do:

Visit *www.facthound.com*

Type in this code: 9781476539331

 Check out projects, games and lots more at
www.capstonekids.com

31

INDEX